The
Book of
Quoems

The
Book of
Quoems

2 Words, 2 Quotes

TIMOTHY J. DONOVAN JR.

THE BOOK OF QUOEMS
2 WORDS, 2 QUOTES

iUniverse books may be ordered through booksellers or by contacting:

iUniverse
1663 Liberty Drive
Bloomington, IN 47403
www.iuniverse.com
1-800-Authors (1-800-288-4677)

Because of the dynamic nature of the Internet, any web addresses or links contained in this book may have changed since publication and may no longer be valid. The views expressed in this work are solely those of the author and do not necessarily reflect the views of the publisher, and the publisher hereby disclaims any responsibility for them.

Any people depicted in stock imagery provided by Getty Images are models, and such images are being used for illustrative purposes only. Certain stock imagery © Getty Images.

ISBN: 978-1-5320-6602-3 (sc)
ISBN: 978-1-5320-6603-0 (e)

Library of Congress Control Number: 2019900573

Print information available on the last page.

iUniverse rev. date: 04/22/2019

This book is dedicated to my wife Janet,
my life long companion,
who inspirers me every day.

A "Quoem"

The Rhyming of Quotes
to form poetic verse,
the piece is titled
to tie the ideas together,
and the result is pure
"Quoetry"

For example;

Opposite Ages

Every sweet has its sour; every evil its good.

Ralph Waldo Emerson (1803 - 1882)

If the young only knew; if the old only could.

French Proverb

Introduction

Welcome to The Book of Quoems, where quotes, proverbs and sayings are turned into poetry and titled as a stand-alone verse. It is a collection of ideas from the famous to the unknown, created long ago to present day and when combined may be complimentary, contradictory, amusing, complete nonsense or take on a new meaning, which may be contrary to the original thought. A Quoem is created by finding two quotes that rhyme and titling it with two words. The first word reflects the idea of the first quote while the second word coincides with the second quote and the result is, a Quoem.

For example:

a.   Start with a Quote:
> **One hand washes the other.**
> Seneca (5 BC -AD65)

b.   Find another that rhymes with the first:
> **One good turn deserves another.**
> Gaius Petronius (-AD 66)

c.   Title it with two words;
Note: When titling, the word cannot be found in the quote.

1.   the first word of the title coincides with the first quote:
> **One hand washes the other.** = ***Collaborative***
> Seneca (5 BC -AD 65)

2. the second word of the title coincides with the second quote:
   One good turn deserves another. = ***Justice***
   Gaius Petronius (~AD 66)

There you have it, a Quoem:

Collaborative Justice

One hand washes the other.
Seneca (5 BC – AD 65)
One good turn deserves another.
Gaius Petronius (~AD 66)

Now that you know what a Quoem is, let me tell you how I created the concept. I have been writing songs and poems most of my life, more songs than poems, so I guess I am more a lyricist than a poet, but one day after writing a new song that ended with a famous quote, I thought it would be a good idea to write an entire song with nothing but famous quotes. During this pursuit, I found that after reading two quotes together that had a poetic rhythm and interesting insights to life, eureka! I had stumbled on something new and at the same time, quite profound. Each one a piece of art, needing nothing more than a title to complete the work. Although that song has yet to be written, what has evolved is this collection of what I call, "The Book of Quoems". While formatting this book, I thought of placing these quoems in some type of order, grouping them into categories such as;

"Famous Individuals" - *there are so many.*

Commemorating Strength

Praising what is lost makes the remembrance dear.
William Shakespeare (1564 - 1616)
Courage is the power of the mind to overcome fear.
Martin Luther King Jr. (1929 - 1968)

or; the "Same Person" - *surprising how many I found.*

Completely Alone

Well done is better than well said.
>   Benjamin Franklin (1706 - 1790)
Three may keep a secret, if two of them are dead.
>   Benjamin Franklin (1706 - 1790)

or "Titling Opposites" - *opposing ideas.*

Abstain Gain

When in doubt, do without.
>   Hofni Samuel (died 1034)
You must lose a fly to catch a trout.
>   George Herbert (1593 - 1633)

or "No individual credit" - *we don't know who said it first.*

Open Transaction

A closed mind is a good thing to lose.
>   Anonymous
Buy on the rumor; sell on the news.
>   Wall Street Proverb

I decided not to categorize them into groups, that a random selection was the best format. Now that you have a good understanding of what Quoems are all about, read the rest of the collection in no particular order. Search for that one gem that will stop you in your tracks, force you to read it again and stay with you forever. Knowing that a quote may be the result of the wisdom of very complicated ideas packaged simply into a single phrase. The Queom take the phrase and title's it with one word and then does it a second time with a rhyme. It is the ultimate solidification of thought, combining literature, vocabulary, poetry and philosophy. But what's better than talking about Queoms? Reading them, of course. Enjoy.

Precise Action

Do not say a little in many words but a great deal in a few.
Pythagoras (582 BC - 507 BC)
You can't build a reputation on what you are going to do.
Henry Ford (1863 - 1947)

Raging Bull

Anger is the feeling that makes your mouth work faster than your mind.
Evan Esar (1899 - 1995)
The man who comes with a tale about others has himself an ax to grind.
Chinese proverb

Observant One

Better be wise by the misfortunes of others than by your own.
Aesop (620 BC - 560 BC)
The strongest man in the world is the man who stands alone.
Thomas H. Huxley (1825 - 1895)

Unsuccessful Shame

Every man is guilty of all the good he didn't do.
Voltaire (1694 - 1778)
Man is the only animal that blushes - or needs to.
Mark Twain (1835 - 1910)

Effective Influence

Much speech is one thing, well-timed speech is another.
Sophocles (496 BC - 406 BC)
Leadership and learning are indispensable to each other.
John F. Kennedy (1917 - 1963)

Frequently Deprived

The impossible is often the untried.
Jim Goodwin
Justice delayed is democracy denied.
Robert F. Kennedy (1925 - 1968)

Frugal Sidestep

The mint makes it first, it is up to you to make it last.
Evan Esar (1899 - 1995)
The girl with a future avoids a man with a past.
Evan Esar (1899 - 1995)

Resonating Result

A bird does not sing because it has an answer.
It sings because it has a song.
Chinese Proverb
We are bits of stellar matter that got cold by accident,
bits of a star gone wrong.
Sir Arthur Eddington (1882 - 1944)

Commendable Collection

There is an applause superior to that of the multitudes: one's own.

Elizabeth Elton Smith (1805-1854)

Nothing of me is original. I am the combined effort of everybody I've ever known.

Chuck Palahniuk (1962 -)

Consider Curiosity

Shallow men believe in luck. Strong men believe in cause and effect.

Ralph Waldo Emerson (1803 - 1882)

If you would persuade, you must appeal to interest rather than intellect.

Benjamin Franklin (1706 - 1790)

Instant Companion

A love that can last forever takes but a second to come about.

Cuban Proverb

A friend is one who walks in when the rest of the world walks out.

Anonymous

Hearing Deprive

You should listen to your heart, and not the voices in your head.

Matt Groening (1954 -)

We simply rob ourselves when we make presents to the dead.

Publilius Syrus (~100 BC)

Select Release

The key to your universe is that you can choose.
Carl Frederick

Train yourself to let go of the things you fear to lose.
George Lucas (1944 -)

Therapeutic Diversion

The only cure for grief is action.
George Henry Lewes (1817 - 1878)

Hard work's a good distraction.
Scott Westerfeld (1963 -)

Sarcastically Amused

The cynics are right nine times out of ten.
Henry Louis Mencken (1880 - 1956)

The only really happy folk are married women and single men.
Henry Louis Mencken (1880 - 1956)

Choice Surplus

If people did not prefer reaping to sowing,
there would not be a hungry person in the land.
Author Unknown

Advice is the only commodity on the market
where the supply always exceeds the demand.
Author Unknown

Relaxing Motion

Take rest; a field that has rested gives a bountiful crop.
Ovid (43 BC – AD 17)
It does not matter how slowly you go so long as you do not stop.
Confucius (551 BC - 479 BC)

Lamenting Effect

We need never be ashamed of our tears.
Charles Dickens (1812 - 1870)
A minute's success pays the failure of years.
Robert Browning (1812 - 1889)

Calm Conflict

Peace is when time doesn't matter as it passes by.
Maria Schell (1926 - 2005)
When the rich wage war it's the poor who die.
Jean-Paul Sartre (1905 - 1980)

Focusing Amount

What we see depends mainly on what we look for.
John Lubbock (1834 - 1913)
I just need enough to tide me over until I need more.
Bill Hoest

Blind Sight

Living is easy with eyes closed, misunderstanding all you see.
John Lennon (1940 - 1980)

I saw the angel in the marble and carved until, I set him free.
Michelangelo Buonarroti (1475 - 1564)

Croon Quickly

It is impossible to experience one's death objectively and still carry a tune.
Woody Allen (1935 -)

Life is full of misery, loneliness, and suffering and it's all over much too soon.
Woody Allen (1935 -)

Act Fast

If opportunity doesn't knock, build a door.
Milton Berle (1908 - 2002)

Fools rush in where fools have been before.
Unknown

Deliberate Intuition

Don't break your shin on a stool that is not in your way.
Irish Proverb

A mother understands what a child does not say.
Jewish Proverb

Empty Choice

Character is what you have left when you've lost everything you can lose.

Evan Esar (1899 - 1995)

When a man tells you that he got rich through hard work, ask him: 'Whose?'

Don Marquis (1878 - 1937)

Clever After

The heart is wiser than the intellect.

Unknown

Travel is only glamorous in retrospect.

Paul Theroux (1941 -)

Diverted Doubt

The really happy person is one who can enjoy the scenery when on a detour.

Unknown

**A man with a watch knows what time it is.
A man with two watches is never sure.**

Segal's Law

Remorseful Transgression

Guilt is a rope that wears thin.

Ayn Rand (1905 - 1982)

Ignorance is not innocence but sin.

Robert Browning (1812 - 1889)

Passionately Proceed

In America sex is an obsession, in other parts of the world it is a fact.
Marlene Dietrich (1901 - 1992)

Before you act consider; when you have considered, tis fully time to act.
Sallust (86 BC - 34 BC)

Inevitable Negotiations

Californians invented the concept of life-style.
This alone warrants their doom.
Don DeLillo (1936 -)

Never hold discussions with the monkey
when the organ grinder is in the room.
Sir Winston Churchill (1874 - 1965)

Alas Ajar

Just think of the tragedy of teaching children not to doubt.
Clarence Darrow (1857 - 1938)

I believe in an open mind, but not so open that your brains fall out.
Arthur Hays Sulzberger (1891 - 1968)

Minor Offering

Justice is incidental to law and order.
J. Edgar Hoover (1895 - 1972)

He is brought as a lamb to the slaughter.
Bible, *Isaiah liii. 7.*

Advancing Retreat

By learning you will teach; by teaching you will learn.
Latin Proverb
Cherish each hour of this day for it can never return.
Og Mandino (1923 - 1996)

Justifiably Weird

Ambition is a poor excuse for not having sense enough to be lazy.
Edgar Bergen (1903 - 1978)
There is no salvation in becoming adapted to a world which is crazy.
Henry Miller (1891 - 1980)

Intended Rest

If you listened hard enough the first time, you might have heard what I meant to say.
Unknown
Better to get up late and be wide awake than to get up early and be asleep all day.
Anonymous

Act After

I must lose myself in action, lest I wither in despair.
Lord Tennyson (1809 - 1892)
I tend to live in the past because most of my life is there.
Herb Caen (1916 - 1997)

Occasionally Reversed

I don't necessarily agree with everything I say.
Marshall McLuhan (1911 - 1980)

If you look back, you'll soon be going that way.
American Proverb

Power Chief

If you wish to know what a man is, place him in authority.
Yugoslav Proverb

Getting in touch with your true self must be your first priority.
Tom Hopkins

Excessively Departed

Do not remove a fly from your friend's forehead with a hatchet.
Chinese Proverb

A spoken word is not a sparrow. Once it flies out, you can't catch it.
Russian Proverb

Mainly Location

Most people are good. They may not be saints, but they are good.
Jimmy Wales (1966 -)

Love thy neighbor as yourself, but choose your neighborhood.
Louise Beal

Successful Wager

You may have to fight a battle more than once to win it.
> Margaret Thatcher (1925 - 2013)

Honesty is the best policy -when there is money in it.
> Mark Twain (1835 - 1910)

Solitary Matters

To be alone is to be different, to be different is to be alone.
> Suzanne Gordon

A man's dying is more the survivors' affair than his own.
> Thomas Mann (1875 - 1955)

Gathering Uncertainty

Each generation will reap what the former generation has sown.
> Chinese Proverb

All we know is still infinitely less than all that remains unknown.
> William Harvey (1578 - 1657)

Educated Windfall

My father taught me to work; he did not teach me to love it.
> Abraham Lincoln (1809 - 1865)

I'm a great believer in luck, and I find the harder I work the more I have of it.
> Thomas Jefferson (1743 - 1826)

Disconnect Ignition

There is always more misery among the lower classes than there is humanity in the higher.

Victor Hugo (1802 - 1885)

Success is not the result of spontaneous combustion. You must set yourself on fire.

Reggie Leach

Assisted Suicide

The best way to convince a fool that he is wrong is to let him have his own way.

Josh Billings (1818 - 1885)

There are many who dare not kill themselves for fear of what the neighbors will say.

Cyril Connolly (1903 - 1974)

Continued Chase

The greatest use of life is to spend it for something that will outlast it.

William James (1842 - 1910)

Most men pursue pleasure with such breathless haste that they hurry past it.

Soren Kierkegaard (1813 - 1855)

Bold Rule

One man with courage makes a majority.

Andrew Jackson (1767 - 1845)

No moral system can rest solely on authority.

A. J. Ayer (1910 - 1989)

Negotiate Immediately

Make your bargain before beginning to plow.
Arab Proverb
Do what's right. Do it right. Do it right now.
Barry Forbes

Questioning Addiction

To philosophize is to doubt.
Michel de Montaigne (1533 - 1592)
Creativity is a drug I cannot live without.
Cecil B. DeMille (1881 - 1959)

Journey Together

Little by little, one travels far.
J. R. R. Tolkien (1892 - 1973)
Hitch your wagon to a star.
Ralph Waldo Emerson (1803 - 1882)

Visionary Recognition

Don't be afraid to see what you see.
Ronald Reagan (1911 - 2004)
Can I ever know you Or you know me?
Sara Teasdale (1884 - 1933)

Educated Pause

Those that know, do. Those that understand, teach.
Aristotle (384 BC - 322 BC)

Well-timed silence hath more eloquence than speech.
Martin Fraquhar Tupper

Dangerous Speed

For most folks, no news is good news;
for the press, good news is not news.
Gloria Borger (1952 -)

A lie can travel halfway round the world
while the truth is putting on its shoes.
Mark Twain (1835 - 1910)

Calmly Continue

Don't take life too seriously. You'll never get out of it alive.
Elbert Hubbard (1856 - 1915)

I think that little by little I'll be able to solve my problems and survive.
Frida Kahlo (1907 - 1954)

Targeting Intellect

It is not enough to aim; you must hit.
Italian Proverb

Insanity destroys reason, but not wit.
Nathaniel Emmons (1745 - 1840)

Disguised Communicator

Wisdom oft lurks beneath a tattered coat.
Caecilius Statius (220 BC - 168 BC)
A good listener is a good talker with a sore throat.
Katharine Whitehorn (1928 -)

Attempting Possibilities

I show up. I listen. I try to laugh.
Anna Quindlen (1953 -)
The universe will reward you for taking risks on its behalf.
Shakti Gawain (1948 -)

Jeopardize Prize

If you don't risk anything you risk even more.
Erica Jong (1942 -)
If winning isn't everything, why do they keep score?
Vince Lombardi (1913 - 1970)

Protective Persona

You can go a long way with a smile.
You can go a lot farther with a smile and a gun.
Al Capone (1899 - 1947)
After I'm dead I'd rather have people ask why
I have no monument than why I have one.
Cato the Elder (234 BC - 149 BC)

Speed Sign

Candy Is dandy but liquor Is quicker.
Ogden Nash (1902 - 1971)

There's a difference between a philosophy and a bumper sticker.
Charles M. Schulz (1922 - 2000)

Yearning After

My motto is: Contented with little, yet wishing for more.
Charles Lamb (1775 - 1834)

The end always passes judgment on what has gone before.
Publilius Syrus (~100 BC)

Inconvenient Forecast

**Until you've lost your reputation,
you never realize what a burden it was.**
Margaret Mitchell (1900 - 1949)

**I violated the Noah rule: Predicting rain doesn't count;
building arks does.**
Warren Buffett (1930 -)

Liberated View

When I discover who I am, I'll be free.
Ralph Ellison (1914 - 1994)

The more opinions you have, the less you see.
Wim Wenders (1945 -)

Challenging Position

Cowards falter, but danger is often overcome by those who nobly dare.

Queen Elizabeth

Even if you're on the right track, you'll get run over if you just sit there.

Will Rogers (1879 - 1935)

Surrogate Shift

Outside show is a poor substitute for inner worth.

Unknown

Give me where to stand, and I will move the earth.

Archimedes (287 BC - 212 BC)

Accidentally Altered

Bore: a man who is never unintentionally rude.

Oscar Wilde (1854 - 1900)

If you can't change your fate, change your attitude.

Amy Tan (1952 -)

Quickly Drained

Happiness makes up in height for what it lacks in length.

Robert Frost (1874 - 1963)

Worry does not empty tomorrow of sorrow, it empties today of strength.

Corrie ten Boom (1892 - 1983)

Occurring Wish

We don't get offered crises, they arrive.
Elizabeth Janeway (1913 - 2005)

One must desire something to be alive.
Margaret Deland (1857 - 1945)

Believing Excellence

In the province of the mind, what one believes to be true either is true or becomes true.
John Lilly

Good writing takes more than just time;
it wants your best moments and the best of you.
Real Live Preacher

Size Comparison

Better to have loved and lost a short
person than never to have loved a tall.
David Chambless

Broadly speaking, the short words are the best,
and the old words best of all.
Sir Winston Churchill (1874 - 1965)

Dense Fear

An intelligence service is, in fact, a stupidity service.
E.B. White

The sad truth is that excellence makes people nervous.
Shana Alexander (1925 - 2005)

Desired Nap

Every man is like the company he is wont to keep.
Euripides (484 BC - 406 BC)
To achieve the impossible dream, try going to sleep.
Joan Klempner

Existing Offer

Take away the miseries and you take away some folks' reason for living.
Toni Cade Bambara (1939 - 1995)
In the long run, we get no more than we have been willing to risk giving.
Sheldon Kopp (1929 - 1999)

Abandon Expression

**If I could get my membership fee back,
I'd resign from the human race.**
Fred Allen (1894 - 1956)
**My evening visitors, if they cannot see the clock,
should find the time in my face.**
Ralph Waldo Emerson (1803 - 1882)

Gradual Change

God's mill grinds slow but sure.
Herbert
Every artist was first an amateur.
Ralph Waldo Emerson (1803 - 1882)

On-going Oath

A contented mind is a continual feast.
> American Proverb

He that promises most will perform least.
> Gaelic Proverb

Adolescent Pursuit

The foundation of every state is the education of its youth.
> Diogenes Laertius (3rd century AD)

When a thing is funny, search it carefully for a hidden truth.
> George Bernard Shaw (1856 - 1950)

Imaginary Stand

The picture you have in your mind of what you're about will come true.
> Bob Dylan (1941 -)

Our greatest glory is not in never falling, but in getting up every time we do.
> Confucius (551 BC - 479 BC)

Missing Ingredient

There is no wisdom without love.
> N. Sri Ram

Sometimes you gotta create what you want to be a part of.
> Geri Weitzman

Past Insecurities

Bygone troubles are a pleasure to talk about.
Yiddish Proverb

Worries go down better with soup than without.
Jewish Proverb

Contrary Course

You must believe in God in spite of what the clergy say.
Benjamin Jowett (1817 - 1893)

I'm an idealist. I don't know where I'm going, but I'm on my way.
Carl Sandburg (1878 - 1967)

Unknowing Interaction

Unless you believe, you will not understand.
Saint Augustine (354 AD - 430 AD)

Those who believe in telekinetics, raise my hand.
Kurt Vonnegut (1922 - 2007)

Apprehensive Tranquility

If you look at life one way, there is always cause for alarm.
Elizabeth Bowen (1899 - 1973)

Don't think there are no crocodiles because the water is calm.
Malayan Proverb

Burn Slow

Love is an exploding cigar we willingly smoke.
Lynda Barry (1956 -)
He who laughs last is generally the last to get the joke.
Terry Cohen

Neither Size

This isn't right. This isn't even wrong.
Wolfgang Pauli (1900 - 1958)
I feel like a tiny bird with a big song!
Jerry Van Amerongen

Simply Ignite

Everyone believes very easily whatever they fear or desire.
Jean de La Fontaine (1621 - 1695)
Education is not the filling of a pail, but the lighting of a fire.
W. B. Yeats (1865 – 1939)

Delaying Development

Learn to labour and to wait.
Henry Wadsworth Longfellow (1807 - 1882)
He enjoys true leisure who has time to improve his soul's estate.
Henry David Thoreau (1817 - 1862)

Altering Therapy

Get your facts first, and then you can distort them as much as you please.

Mark Twain (1835 - 1910)

The art of medicine consists in amusing the patient while nature cures the disease.

Voltaire (1694 - 1778)

Skillfully Historic

Don't rule out working with your hands. It does not preclude using your head.

Andy Rooney (1919 - 2011)

I don't think anyone should write their autobiography until after they're dead.

Samuel Goldwyn (1882 - 1974)

Existing Thought

Conscience is God's presence in man.

Emanuel Swedenborg (1688 - 1772)

They can do all because they think they can.

Virgil (70 BC - 19 BC)

Captive Alternative

How helpless we are, like netted birds, when we are caught by desire!

Belva Plain (1915 - 2010)

We feel free when we escape, even if it be but from the frying pan to the fire.

Eric Hoffer (1902 - 1983)

Motivation Liberation

The Creator has not given you a longing to do
that which you have no ability to do.

Orison Swett Marden (1850 - 1924)

Acquire inner peace and a multitude
will find their salvation near you.

Catherine de Hueck Doherty (1896 - 1985)

Unspoken Capacity

Our lives begin to end the day we become silent
about things that matter.

Martin Luther King Jr. (1929 - 1968)

The length of a film should be directly related to
the endurance of the human bladder.

Alfred Hitchcock (1899 - 1980)

Dangling Fix

Life resembles the banquet of Damocles; the sword is ever
suspended.

Voltaire (1694 - 1778)

Glass, china, and reputation are easily cracked, and never well
mended.

Benjamin Franklin (1706 - 1790)

Believe Equally

Put more trust in nobility of character than in an oath.

Solon (638 BC - 559 BC)

Justice cannot be for one side alone, but must be for both.

Eleanor Roosevelt (1884 - 1962)

Attitude Adjustment

I have a new philosophy. I'm only going to dread one day at a time.

Charles M. Schulz (1922 - 2000)

Soar, eat ether, see what has never been seen; depart, be lost, but climb.

Edna St. Vincent Millay (1892 - 1950)

Clean Behavior

The classes that wash most are those that work least.

G.K. Chesterton (1874 - 1936)

Bear in mind that you should conduct yourself in life as at a feast.

Epictetus (55 AD - 135 AD)

Mostly Nonsense

Ninety percent of everything is crap.

Theodore Sturgeon (1918 - 1985)

In politics, absurdity is not a handicap.

Napoleon Bonaparte (1769 - 1821)

Feminine Faux-pas

Women! Can't live with them...pass the beer nuts.

Norm (Cheers)

Some of the worst mistakes of my life have been haircuts.

Jim Morrison (1943 - 1971)

Beyond Understanding

**An intellectual is a man who takes more words than necessary
to tell more than he knows.**

> Dwight D. Eisenhower (1890 - 1969)

**We must learn to be still in the midst of activity
and to be vibrantly alive in repose.**

> Indira Gandhi (1917 - 1984)

Double Trouble

**If an idea's worth having once,
it's worth having twice.**

> Tom Stoppard (1937 -)

**Three failures denote uncommon strength.
A weakling has not enough grit to fail thrice.**

> Minna Thomas Antrim (1861 - 1950)

Timetable Companions

A schedule defends from chaos and whim.

> Annie Dillard (1945 -)

Abuse a man unjustly, and you will make friends for him.

> Edgar Watson Howe (1853 - 1937)

Focused Development

**The world stands aside to let anyone pass
who knows where he is going.**

> David Starr Jordan (1851 - 1931)

**If every day is an awakening, you will never grow old.
You will just keep growing.**

> Gail Sheehy (1937 -)

Party Hardy

Mom always tells me to celebrate everyone's uniqueness.
I like the way that sounds.
> Hilary Duff (1987 -)

What's the difference between a boyfriend and a husband?
About 30 pounds.
> Cindy Gardner

Injured Earnings

Discouragement is simply the despair of wounded self-love.
> Francois de Fenelon (1651 - 1715)

A large income is the best recipe for happiness I ever heard of.
> Jane Austen (1775 - 1817)

Not Angel-like

Words without thoughts never to heaven go.
> William Shakespeare (1564 - 1616)

Moral indignation is jealousy with a halo.
> H. G. Wells (1866 - 1946)

Tiny Identity

A person's a person, no matter how small.
> Dr. Seuss (1904 - 1991)

Learning to love yourself is the greatest love of all.
> Michael Masser and Linda Creed

Evoking Joy

God gave us memory so that we might have roses in December.
James M. Barrie (1860 - 1937)
Happiness isn't something you experience; it's something you remember.
Oscar Levant (1906 - 1972)

Foundation Realization

Self-respect is the cornerstone of all virtue.
John Herschel (1792 - 1871)
When there is no enemy within, the enemies outside cannot hurt you.
African proverb

Con Test

In order to preserve your self-respect,
it is sometimes necessary to lie and cheat.
Robert Byrne
Where it is a duty to worship the sun
it is pretty sure to be a crime to examine the laws of heat.
John Viscount Morley (1838 - 1923)

Improved Independence

It is almost impossible to smile on the outside
without feeling better on the inside.
Author Unknown
No fear. No distractions.
The ability to let that which does not matter truly slide.
Chuck Palahniuk (1962 -)

Left Unique

**A man is rich in proportion to the number of things
he can afford to let alone.**

Henry David Thoreau (1817 - 1862)

**Part of being a Master is learning how to sing in nobody else's
voice but your own.**

Hugh Macleod

Pointless Offering

Don't need to say please to no man for a happy tune.

Neil Diamond (1941 -)

Beware the flatterer: he feeds you with an empty spoon.

Cosino DeGregrio

Conflict Within

Do or do not. There is no try.

Yoda

Our remedies oft in ourselves do lie.

William Shakespeare (1564 - 1616)

Instinctively Specific

Men are born to succeed, not fail.

Henry David Thoreau (1817 - 1862)

We think in generalities, but we live in detail.

Alfred North Whitehead (1861 - 1947)

Poised Weary

We confide in our strength, without boasting of it;
we respect that of others, without fearing it.

Thomas Jefferson (1743 - 1826)

A platitude is simply a truth repeated
until people get tired of hearing it.

Stanley Baldwin (1867 - 1947)

Lost Release

If you can find a path with no obstacles,
it probably doesn't lead anywhere.

Frank A. Clark

Under certain circumstances, profanity
provides a relief denied even to prayer.

Mark Twain (1835 - 1910)

Corporate Choice

In this business you either sink or swim or you don't.

David Smith

I have a higher and grander standard of principle than
George Washington. He could not lie; I can, but I won't.

Mark Twain (1835 - 1910)

Innocent Encounter

The eyes are not responsible
when the mind does the seeing.

Publilius Syrus (~100 BC)

The opportunity for brotherhood presents itself every time
you meet a human being.

Jane Wyman (1917 -2007)

Random Participation

Though I am not naturally honest,
I am so sometimes by chance.

William Shakespeare (1564 - 1616)

Life may not be the party we hoped for,
but while we're here we should dance.

Unknown

Passionate Thoughts

Love is that splendid triggering of human vitality.

Jose Ortega y Gasset (1883 - 1955)

Imagination is the one weapon in the war against reality.

Jules de Gaultier (1858 - 1942)

Averted Danger

A stumble may prevent a fall.

English Proverb

The policy of being too cautious is the greatest risk of all.

Jawaharlal Nehru (1889 - 1964)

Stagnant Progression

Consistency requires you to be as ignorant today as you were a year ago.

Bernard Berenson (1865 - 1959)

Develop a passion for learning. If you do, you will never cease to grow.

Anthony J. D'Angelo

Chance Commitment

Take calculated risks.
That is quite different from being rash.

George S. Patton (1885 - 1945)

Marriage is not just spiritual communion,
it is also remembering to take out the trash.

Dr. Joyce Brothers (1927 - 2013)

Absent Distrust

Writers should be read, but neither seen nor heard.

Daphne du Maurier (1907 - 1989)

Doubt is not a pleasant condition, but certainty is absurd.

Voltaire (1694 - 1778)

Start Sweetheart

Whatever you can do or dream, begin it.

Johann Wolfgang von Goethe (1749 - 1832)

Love much. Earth has enough of bitter in it.

Ella Wheeler Wilcox (1850 - 1919)

Profitable Distance

Only sick music makes money today.

Friedrich Nietzsche (1844 - 1900)

Brass bands are all very well in their place
outdoors and several miles away.

Sir Thomas Beecham (1879 - 1961)

Harvesting Expenses

Whatsoever a man soweth, that shall he also reap.
Bible

You'd be surprised how much it costs to look this cheap.
Dolly Parton (1946 -)

Spaciously Tight

There is always room for a man of force,
and he makes room for many.
Ralph Waldo Emerson (1803 - 1882)

The easiest way for your children to learn about money
is for you not to have any.
Katharine Whitehorn (1928 -)

Core Emotion

To pull together is to avoid being pulled apart.
Bob Allisat

We know truth, not only by reason, but also by the heart.
Blaise Pascal (1623 - 1662)

Diverse Deserter

All marriages are mixed marriages.
Chantal Saperstein

I feel like a fugitive from the law of averages.
William H. Mauldin (1921 - 2003)

Experience Relaxation

I am never afraid of what I know.
> Anna Sewell (1820 - 1878)

A clear conscience is a good pillow.
> American Proverb

Uncharitable Future

Many people despise wealth, but few know how to give it away.
> Francois de La Rochefoucauld (1613 - 1680)

Sure I'm for helping the elderly. I'm going to be old myself some day.
> Lillian Carter (1898 – 1983)

Initially Dry

First things first, but not necessarily in that order.
> Doctor Who

Thousands have lived without love, not one without water.
> W.H. Auden (1907 - 1973)

Speech Impediment

Constantly talking isn't necessarily communicating.
> Charlie Kaufman (1958 -)

The opposite of talking isn't listening.
The opposite of talking is waiting.
> Fran Lebowitz (1950 -)

Cover Support

Do not cut down the tree that gives you shade.
Persian Proverb

Be bold and mighty powers will come to your aid.
Basil King (1859 – 1928)

Postponed Evaluation

Never think that God's delays are God's denials.
Comte de Buffon (1707 - 1788)

**The gem cannot be polished without friction,
nor man perfected without trials.**
Chinese Proverb

Quiet Desire

Silence is golden when you can't think of a good answer.
Muhammad Ali (1942 - 2016)

**I would not know what the spirit of a philosopher might wish
more to be, than a good dancer.**
Friedrich Nietzsche (1844 - 1900)

Dead Reckoning

**Death is more universal than life;
everyone dies but not everyone lives.**
A. Sachs

**If there be any truer measure of a man than by what he does,
it must be by what he gives.**
Robert South (1634 - 1716)

Traveling Youth

Walking is the best possible exercise.
Habituate yourself to walk very far.
Thomas Jefferson (1743 - 1826)

I wonder what it means when your
grandson is more crotchety than you are.
Aaron McGruder (1974 -)

Target Tranquility

The wisest men follow their own direction.
Euripides (484 BC - 406 BC)

Man seeketh in society comfort, use and protection.
Sir Francis Bacon (1561 - 1626)

Traveling Motionless

My driving abilities from Mexico have helped me get through
Hollywood.
Salma Hayek (1966 -)

Far from idleness being the root of all evil, it is rather the only
true good.
Soren Kierkegaard (1813 - 1855)

Fancy Timing

We have got to have a dream if we are going to make a dream
come true.
Denis Waitley

Three o'clock is always too late or too early for anything you
want to do.
Jean-Paul Sartre (1905 - 1980)

Passing Payment

Life is a sexually transmitted disease.
> R. D. Laing (1927 - 1989)

God heals, and the doctor takes the fees.
> Benjamin Franklin (1706 - 1790)

Illuminating Respect

There is no new thing under the sun.
> Bible

Whatever you are, be a good one.
> Abraham Lincoln (1809 - 1865)

Negative Charge

To play it safe is not to play.
> Robert Altman (1925 - 2007)

Feel the fear and do it anyway.
> Susan Jeffers (1938 - 2012)

Brief Chief

Short is the joy that guilty pleasure brings.
> Euripides (484 BC - 406 BC)

Management is doing things right; leadership is doing the right things.
> Peter Drucker (1909 - 2005)

Ease After

**Too often we... enjoy the comfort of opinion
without the discomfort of thought.**

John F. Kennedy (1917 - 1963)

**Do not seek to follow in the footsteps of the men of old;
seek what they sought.**

Basho

Lacking Fear

**Every man without passions has within him no principle of action,
nor motive to act.**

Claude A. Helvetius (1715 - 1771)

**Be not afraid of life. Believe that life is worth living, and your belief
will help create the fact.**

William James (1842 - 1910)

Immediately Postponed

**Successful leaders have the courage to take action where others
hesitate.**

Author Unknown

**You know you're getting old when it takes too much effort to
procrastinate.**

Unknown

Targeted Possession

Stoop and you'll be stepped on; stand tall and you'll be shot at.

Carlos A. Urbizo

**All that really belongs to us is time; even he who has nothing
else has that.**

Baltasar Gracian (1601 - 1658)

Amusing Split

Nothing shows a man's character more than what he laughs at.
Johann Wolfgang von Goethe (1749 - 1832)

**There is one thing I would break up over, and that is
if she caught me with another woman. I won't stand for that.**
Steve Martin (1945 -)

Meager Smile

It is the sign of a weak mind to be unable to bear wealth.
Seneca (5 BC - 65 AD)

...happiness gives us the energy which is the basis of health.
Henri-Frédéric Amiel (1821 - 1881)

Treasured Insight

A book holds a house of gold.
Chinese Proverb

Eyes that see do not grow old.
Nicaraguan Proverb

Accomplished Companion

**You have succeeded in life when all you really want
is only what you really need.**
Vernon Howard (1918 - 1992)

**Outside of a dog, a book is man's best friend.
Inside of a dog it's too dark to read.**
Groucho Marx (1890 - 1977)

Obligation Destination

Property has its duties as well as its rights.
Thomas Brummond
If suffer we must, let's suffer on the heights.
Victor Hugo (1802 - 1885)

Restful Decision

Yet a little sleep, a little slumber,
a little folding of the hands to sleep.
Bible, *Proverbs xxiv. 33.*
Creativity is allowing yourself to make mistakes.
Art is knowing which ones to keep.
Scott Adams (1957 -)

Clever Departure

Not by wrath does one kill, but by laughter.
Friedrich Nietzsche (1844 - 1900)
Speak the truth, but leave immediately after.
Slovenian Proverb

Deceptive Selection

A great deal of intelligence can be invested in ignorance
when the need for illusion is deep.
Saul Bellow (1915 - 2005)
We are rich only through what we give;
and poor only through what we refuse and keep.
Madame Swetchine (1782 - 1857)

Finding Forever

There is no shortage of good days.
It is good lives that are hard to come by.
Annie Dillard (1945 -)

To achieve great things we must live as though
we were never going to die.
Marquis de Vauvenargues (1715 - 1747)

Everlasting Roar

My friend is one... who take me for what I am.
Henry David Thoreau (1817 - 1862)

It's better to live one day as a lion
than a hundred years as a lamb.
John Gotti (1940 - 2002)

Welcomed Truth

Hay is more acceptable to an ass than gold.
Latin Proverb

An honest tale speeds best, being plainly told.
William Shakespeare (1564 - 1616)

Individually Acquired

My father used to say, 'Let them see you and not the suit.
That should be secondary.'
Cary Grant (1904 - 1986)

When we are planning for posterity, we ought to remember that
virtue is not hereditary.
Thomas Paine (1737 - 1809)

Added Persuasion

Arithmetic is being able to count up to twenty without taking off your shoes.
Mickey Mouse (1928 -)

Success is a lousy teacher. It seduces smart people into thinking they can't lose.
Bill Gates (1955 -)

Cautiously Just

Love all, trust a few. Do wrong to none.
William Shakespeare (1564 - 1616)

After thirty nine years this is all I've done.
Dylan Thomas (1914 - 1953)

Placed Right

I have the heart of a child. I keep it in a jar on my shelf.
Robert Bloch (1917 - 1994)

No price is too high to pay for the privilege of owning yourself.
Friedrich Nietzsche (1844 - 1900)

Mistakenly Laborious

A woman's place is in the wrong.
James Thurber (1894 - 1961)

Instant gratification takes too long.
Carrie Fisher (1956 - 2016)

Cosmos Physician

You have to believe that the universe will provide.
Steve Crosby
Every patient carries her or his own doctor inside.
Albert Schweitzer (1875 - 1965)

Aged Individual

All would live long, but none would be old.
Benjamin Franklin (1706 - 1790)
Nature made him, and then broke the mold.
Ludovico Ariosto (1474 - 1533)

Testimonial Construction

Women are cursed, and men are the proof.
Rosanne Barr (1952-)
**Passion holds up the bottom of the universe
and genius paints up its roof.**
Chang Ch'ao

Constant Fluctuating

We are always the same age inside.
Gertrude Stein (1874 - 1946)
We rise in glory as we sink in pride.
Young

Meager Incentive

I have no faith, very little hope, and as much charity
as I can afford.

Thomas H. Huxley (1825 - 1895)

The avoidance of taxes is the only intellectual pursuit
that carries any reward.

John Maynard Keynes (1883 - 1946)

Recognize Anyone?

He who learns but does not think, is lost!
He who thinks but does not learn is in great danger.

Confucius (551 BC - 479 BC)

Honest criticism is hard to take, particularly from
a relative, a friend, an acquaintance, or a stranger.

Franklin P. Jones

Possessing Views

Winter is on my head, but eternal spring is in my heart.

Victor Hugo (1802 - 1885)

Any clod can have the facts, but having opinions is an art.

Charles McCabe (1915 - 1983)

Celebrated Improvement

Partying is such sweet sorrow.

Robert Byrne

The future will be better tomorrow.

Dan Quayle (1947 -)

Endlessly Futility

Eternity is a mere moment, just long enough for a joke.
Hermann Hesse (1877 - 1962)

Lawyers spend a great deal of their time shoveling smoke.
Oliver Wendell Holmes Jr. (1841 - 1935)

Losing Time

I'm worried that the universe will soon need replacing. It's not holding a charge.
Edward Chilton

A perfect method for adding drama to life is to wait until the deadline looms large.
Alyce P. Cornyn-Selby

Prolonged Deception

I think we might be going a bridge too far.
Sir Frederick Browning (1896 - 1965)

It was beautiful and simple, as truly great swindles are.
O. Henry (1862 - 1910)

Inquisitive Irks

It is a miracle that curiosity survives formal education.
Albert Einstein (1879 - 1955)

I don't have pet peeves, I have whole kennels of irritation.
Whoopi Goldberg (1949 -)

Inverse Adaptability

The minute one utters a certainty, the opposite comes to mind.
May Sarton (1912 - 1995)
Learn not only to find what you like, learn to like what you find.
Anthony J. D'Angelo

Traveling Invention

Gossip needs no carriage.
Russian Proverb
God created sex. Priests created marriage.
Voltaire (1694 - 1778)

Impression Protection

I don't have a photograph, but you can have my footprints. They're upstairs in my socks.
Groucho Marx (1890 - 1977)
Instead of giving a politician the keys to the city, it might be better to change the locks.
Doug Larson (1926 -)

Follow Blindly

By learning to obey, you will know how to command.
Italian Proverb
Baseball is like church. Many attend, few understand.
Leo Durocher (1906 - 1991)

Act Now

Tell me and I'll forget; show me and I may remember;
involve me and I'll understand.

Chinese Proverb

Our main business is not to see what lies dimly at a distance
but to do what lies clearly at hand.

Thomas Carlyle (1795 - 1881)

Redundant Understanding

If an idiot were to tell you the same story every day for a year,
you would end by believing it.

Horace Mann (1796 - 1859)

Rationality is the recognition of the fact that nothing can alter the
truth and nothing can take precedence over that act of perceiving it.

Ayn Rand (1905 - 1982)

Accomplished Evolution

Force has no place where there is need of skill.

Herodotus (484 BC - 430 BC)

The law must be stable, but it must not stand still.

Roscoe Pound (1870 - 1964)

Properly Pleased

It is honorable to be accused by those
who deserve to be accused.

Latin Proverb

Blessed are we who can laugh at ourselves
for we shall never cease to be amused.

Unknown

Common Skeptic

When a dog bites a man, that is not news, because it happens so often.

John B. Bogart (1848 - 1921)

A cynic is a man who, when he smells flowers, looks around for a coffin.

Henry Louis Mencken (1880 - 1956)

Creative Intuition

Practice and thought might gradually forge many an art.

Virgil (70 BC - 19 BC)

We know truth, not only by reason, but also by the heart.

Blaise Pascal (1623 - 1662)

Genuine Achievement

Everything you can imagine is real.

Picasso (1881 - 1973)

If you make the world a little better,
then you have accomplished a great deal.

Unknown

Legislative Address

Any fool can make a rule and any fool will mind it.

Henry David Thoreau (1817 - 1862)

A man travels the world over in search of what he needs and returns home to find it.

George Moore

Changing Resistance

Where there is hatred, let me sow love. Where there is injury, pardon.

Saint Francis of Assisi (1181 - 1226)

We must always change, renew, rejuvenate ourselves; otherwise we harden.

Johann Wolfgang von Goethe (1749 - 1832)

Practicing Justice

Life is like a piano... what you get out of it depends on how you play it.

Unknown

I disapprove of what you say, but I will defend to the death your right to say it.

Voltaire (1694 - 1778)

Crib Death

The Earth is the Cradle of the Mind but one cannot eternally live in a cradle.

Konstantin E. Tsiolkovsky (1857 - 1935)

It is always a silly thing to give advice, but to give good advice is fatal.

Oscar Wilde (1854 - 1900)

Penned Presumption

Learn as much by writing as by reading.

Lord Acton (1834 - 1902)

I'm kind of jealous of the life I'm supposedly leading.

Zach Braff (1975-)

Exceptional Observation

He has achieved success who has lived well, laughed often, and loved much.

Bessie A. Stanley (1879 - 1952)

Every moment is a golden one for him who has the vision to recognize it as such.

Henry Miller (1891 - 1980)

Familiar Performance

We most often go astray on a well trodden and much frequented road.

Seneca (5 BC - 65 AD)

You never know how a horse will pull until you hook him up to a heavy load.

Paul "Bear" Bryant (1913 - 1983)

Achieving Balance

The glory of great men should always be measured by the means they have used to acquire it.

Francois de La Rochefoucauld (1613 - 1680)

A man likes his wife to be just clever enough to comprehend his cleverness, and just stupid enough to admire it.

Israel Zangwill (1864 - 1926)

Astray Companion

People, like nails, lose their effectiveness when they lose direction and begin to bend.

Walter Savage Landor (1775 - 1864)

If you would win a man to your cause, first convince him that you are his sincere friend.

Abraham Lincoln (1809 - 1865)

Familiar Refrain

Trust one who has gone through it.
Virgil (70 BC - 19 BC)

If you don't want anyone to know, don't do it.
Chinese Proverb

Unfavorable Assistance

In adversity remember to keep an even mind.
Horace (65 BC - 8 BC)

Rich gifts wax poor when givers prove unkind.
William Shakespeare (1564 - 1616)

Warm Direction

I can't think of any sorrow in the world that a hot bath wouldn't help, just a little bit.
Susan Glaspell (1876 - 1948)

It is better for civilization to be going down the drain than to be coming up it.
Henry Allen

Missing Price

The only paradise is paradise lost.
Marcel Proust (1871 - 1922)

So far I haven't heard of anybody who wants to stop living on account of the cost.
Kin Hubbard (1868 - 1930)

Considerate Affection

No one is useless in this world
who lightens the burdens of another.

Charles Dickens (1812 - 1870)

The most important thing a father can do for his children
is to love their mother.

Author Unknown

Ultimate Trap

We are always in search of the redeeming formula,
the crystallizing thought.

Etty Hillesum (1914 - 1943)

Laws are spider webs through which the big flies pass
and the little ones get caught.

Honore de Balzac (1799 - 1850)

Undiscovered Treasure

Impossible is a word only to be found in the dictionary of fools.

Napoleon (1769 - 1821)

The words that enlighten the soul are more precious than jewels.

Hazrat Inayat Khan

Belated Recognition

It is cruel to discover one's mediocrity
only when it is too late.

W. Somerset Maugham (1874 - 1965)

If men could only know each other,
they would neither idolize nor hate.

Elbert Hubbard (1856 - 1915)

Fluctuating Fame

The cost of living is going up and the chance of living is going down.

Flip Wilson (1933 - 1998)

I too shall lie in the dust when I am dead, but now let me win noble renown.

Homer (800 BC - 700 BC)

Pastime Punishment

The bow cannot always stand bent, nor can human frailty subsist without some lawful recreation.

Miguel de Cervantes (1547 - 1616)

Children might or might not be a blessing, but to create them and then fail them was surely damnation.

Lois McMaster Bujold (1949 -)

Juvenile Delinquent

Boys will be boys, and so will a lot of middle-aged men.

Kin Hubbard (1868 - 1930)

You can't turn back the clock. But you can wind it up again.

Bonnie Prudden (1914 - 2011)

Doubt Everything

**Each moment in time we have it all,
even when we think we don't.**

Melody Beattie (1948 -)

**Put your whole self into it, and you will find your true voice.
Hold back and you won't.**

Hugh Macleod

Stationary Existence

The need of man to wholly realize himself is the only fixed star.
Arthur Miller (1915 - 2005)
Wanting to be someone you're not is a waste of the person you are.
Kurt Cobain (1967 - 1994)

Anxiously Hungry

Liberty means responsibility.
That is why most men dread it.
George Bernard Shaw (1856 - 1950)
We don't know what we want,
but we are ready to bite somebody to get it.
Will Rogers (1879 - 1935)

Quality Decision

The weak can never forgive. Forgiveness is the attribute of the strong.
Mahatma Gandhi (1869 - 1948)
It often requires more courage to dare to do right than to fear to do wrong.
Abraham Lincoln (1809 - 1865)

Choice Enforcement

I would rather be right and die
than be wrong and kill.
Holly Lisle
A person in a uniform is merely an extension
of another person's will.
Philip Slater (1927 - 2013)

Varying Results

In theory, there is no difference between theory and practice;
In practice, there is.

Chuck Reid

Don't be a fool and die for your country.
Let the other sonofabitch die for his.

George S. Patton (1885 - 1945)

Still Done

Never give advice unless asked.

German Proverb

Even God cannot change the past.

Agathon (448 BC - 400 BC)

Fight Bravely

The race is not to the swift, nor the battle to the strong.

Bible, *Ecclesiastes ix. 11.*

To live a creative life, we must lose our fear of being wrong.

Joseph Chilton Pearce (1926 -)

Manual Search

Look like a girl, act like a lady, think like a man
and work like a dog.

Caroline K. Simon (1900 - 1993)

If you don't find it in the index, look very carefully
through the entire catalogue.

Unknown

Indulging Assurance

I have learned not to worry about love;
but to honor its coming with all my heart.

Alice Walker (1944 -)

Confidence is the sexiest thing a woman can have.
It's much sexier than any body part.

Aimee Mullins (1976 -)

Less News

The only thing worse than being talked about is not being talked about.

Oscar Wilde (1854 - 1900)

An ignorant person is one who doesn't know what you have just found out.

Will Rogers (1879 - 1935)

Making Errors

It is through creating, not possessing, that life is revealed.

Vida D. Scudder(1861 - 1954)

An expert is a person who has made all the mistakes that can be made in a very narrow field.

Niels Bohr (1885 - 1962)

Joyous Participation

Success is liking yourself, liking what you do, and liking how you do it.

Maya Angelou (1928 - 2014)

Life is like a sewer... what you get out of it depends on what you put into it.

Tom Lehrer (1928 -)

Creation Hesitation

This is why God invented network television.
Ted Harbert (1955 -)

Once I make up my mind, I'm full of indecision.
Oscar Levant (1906 - 1972)

Contradicting Conclusion

**To deny we need and want power
is to deny that we hope to be effective.**
Liz Smith

**When a thing is done, it's done. Don't look back.
Look forward to your next objective.**
George C. Marshall (1880 - 1959)

Fresh Flora

**We all have big changes in our lives that are more or less
a second chance.**
Harrison Ford (1942 -)

**I'm not a vegetarian because I love animals. I'm a vegetarian
because I hate plants.**
A. Whitney Brown (1952 -)

Confident Speaker

Be bold and mighty powers will come to your aid.
Basil King (1859 - 1928)

The passions are the only orators that always persuade.
Francois de La Rochefoucauld (1613 - 1680)

Vital Understanding

War is just to those to whom war is necessary.
Titus Livius (59 BC – AD 17)

It is impossible to make wisdom hereditary.
Author Unknown

Honestly Expected

When my love swears that she is made of truth, I do believe her, though I know she lies.
William Shakespeare (1564 - 1616)

If all the girls who attended the Yale prom were laid end to end, I wouldn't be a bit surprised.
Dorothy Parker (1893 - 1967)

Enduring Prospective

Have regard for your name, since it will remain for you longer than a great store of gold.
Ecclesiasticus

To be 70 years young is sometimes far more cheerful and hopeful than to be 40 years old.
Oliver Wendell Holmes (1809 - 1894)

Crucial Identification

I know that poetry is indispensable, but to what I could not say.
Jean Cocteau (1889 - 1963)

I don't give a damn for a man that can only spell a word one way.
Mark Twain (1835 - 1910)

Personal Wellbeing

Depend not on another,
but lean instead on thyself.

The laws of Manu

If I knew I was going to live this long,
I'd have taken better care of myself.

Mickey Mantle (1931 - 1995)

Custom Precision

Tradition is a guide and not a jailer.

W. Somerset Maugham (1874 - 1965)

If you are out to describe the truth,
leave elegance to the tailor.

Albert Einstein (1879 - 1955)

Quite Struggle

The eternal silence of these infinite spaces fills me with dread.

Blaise Pascal (1623 – 1662)

It is hard to fight an enemy who has outposts in your head.

Sally Kempton

Immeasurable Turns

An undefined problem has an infinite number of solutions.

Robert A. Humphrey

Revolutions always come around again. That's why they're
called revolutions.

Terry Pratchett

Reflecting Image

I was not lying. I said things that later on seemed to be untrue.
Richard Nixon (1913 - 1994)
When you stare into the abyss the abyss stares back at you.
Friedrich Nietzsche (1844 - 1900)

Accumulative Deception

The great thing about getting older is that you don't lose all the other ages you've been.
Madeleine L'Engle (1918 - 2007)
Of course the game is rigged. Don't let that stop you— if you don't play, you can't win.
Robert Heinlein (1907 - 1988)

Mighty Misleading

Strong beliefs win strong men, and then make them stronger.
Walter Bagehot (1826 - 1877)
The illegal we do immediately. The unconstitutional takes a little longer.
Henry Kissinger (1923 -)

Engineering Madness

Men have become the tools of their tools.
Henry David Thoreau (1817 - 1862)
By their own follies they perished, the fools.
Homer (800 BC - 700 BC)

Intellectual Approach

A man paints with his brains and not with his hands.
Michelangelo Buonarroti (1475 - 1564)

I must create a system, or be enslaved by another man's.
William Blake (1757 - 1827)

Existing Freely

Illusions are art, for the feeling person and it is by art that you live, if you do.
Elizabeth Bowen (1899 - 1973)

Choose your pleasures for yourself and do not let them be imposed upon you.
Lord Chesterfield (1694 - 1773)

Space Exploration

You can't have everything. Where would you put it?
Steven Wright (1955 -)

If we knew what it was we were doing, it would not be called research, would it?
Albert Einstein (1879 - 1955)

Odiferous Request

Fish and visitors smell in three days.
Benjamin Franklin (1706 - 1790)

Prayer does not change God, but changes him who prays.
Soren Kierkegaard (1813 - 1855)

Humbling Trust

Life is a long lesson in humility.

James M. Barrie (1860 - 1937)

The price of greatness is responsibility.

Sir Winston Churchill (1874 - 1965)

Pure Execution

May no portent of evil be attached to the words I say.

Anonymous

It is not enough to do good; one must do it the right way.

John Viscount Morley (1838 - 1923)

Increasingly Cavalier

Never discourage anyone...who continually makes progress, no matter how slow.

Plato (427 BC - 347 BC)

I don't think about risks much. I just do what I want to do. If you gotta go, you gotta go.

Lillian Carter (1898 - 1983)

Sustaining Doubt

Beginning is easy - Continuing is hard.

Japanese Proverb

I'm still an atheist, thank God.

Luis Bunuel (1900 - 1983)

Mysterious Sensation

It is the unknown we fear when we look upon death and
darkness, nothing more.

J. K. Rowling (1965 -)

All you need in this life is ignorance and confidence –
and then success is sure.

Mark Twain (1835 - 1910)

Altering Seize

The universe is change; our life is what our thoughts make it.

Marcus Aurelius Antoninus (AD 121-
AD 180)

The thing women have yet to learn is nobody gives you power.
You just take it.

Roseanne Barr (1952 -)

Limiting Provider

Underpromise; overdeliver.

Tom Peters (1942 -)

I have found that among its other benefits, giving liberates the
soul of the giver.

Maya Angelou (1928 - 2014)

Self Control

A joyful life is an individual creation that cannot be copied from
a recipe.

Mihaly Csikszentmihalyi (1934 -)

We are each responsible for our own life - no other person is or
even can be.

Oprah Winfrey (1954 -)

Hidden Treasure

I adore simple pleasures.
They are the last refuge of the complex.
Oscar Wilde (1854 - 1900)

An intellectual is a person who has discovered
something more interesting than sex.
Aldous Huxley (1894 - 1963)

Made Trade

Foolish writers and readers are created for each other.
Horace Walpole (1717 - 1797)

That's the secret to life... replace one worry with another....
Charles M. Schulz (1922 - 2000)

Enthusiastically Content

How poor are they who have not patience!
What wound did ever heal but by degrees.
William Shakespeare (1564 - 1616)

He that would live in peace and at ease,
must not speak all he knows nor judge all he sees.
Benjamin Franklin (1706 - 1790)

Revealing Results

Our deeds determine us, as much as we determine our deeds.
Marian Evans (1819 - 1880)

From each according to his abilities, to each according to his
needs.
Louis Blanc (1811 - 1882)

Upheaval Challenge

Anyone can revolt.
> Georges Rouault (1871 - 1958)

It is only the first step that is difficult.
> Marie De Vichy-Chaconne

Mathematical Results

Equations are the devil's sentences.
> Stephen Colbert (1964 -)

When anger rises, think of the consequences.
> Confucius (551 BC - 479 BC)

Clever Trade

We can learn much from wise words, little from wisecracks, and less from wise guys.
> William Arthur Ward (1921 - 1994)

When of a gossiping circle it was asked, "What are they doing?" The answer was, "Swapping lies."
> Richard Brinsley Sheridan (1751 - 1816)

Quick Exit

So little time and so little to do.
> Oscar Levant (1906 - 1972)

The best way out is always through.
> Robert Frost (1874 - 1963)

Without Restriction

Never believe anything until it has been officially denied.

Claud Cockburn (1904 - 1981)

He is free knows how to keep in his own hands the power to decide.

Salvador De Madriaga

Genetically Equal

Man's main task in life is to give birth to himself,
to become what he potentially is.

Erich Fromm (1900 - 1980)

There is no king who has not had a slave among his ancestors,
and no slave who has not had a king among his.

Helen Keller (1880 - 1968)

Proportionally Indifferent

Advertising is 85% confusion and 15% commission.

Fred Allen (1894 - 1956)

Women who seek to be equal with men lack ambition.

Timothy Leary (1920 - 1996)

Special Purpose

We don't always get to choose what we love.

Scott Westerfeld (1963 -)

The heart has its reasons which reason knows nothing of.

Blaise Pascal (1623 - 1662)

Ironic Offering

We are suffering from too much sarcasm.

Marianne Moore (1887 - 1972)

If you give your son only one gift, let it be enthusiasm.

Bruce Barton (1886 - 1967)

Unpredictably Frail

Some rise by sin, and some by virtue fall.

William Shakespeare (1564 - 1616)

Love is or it ain't. Thin love ain't love at all.

Toni Morrison (1931 -)

Humble Sincerity

Be modest! It is the kind of pride least likely to offend.

Jules Renard (1864 - 1910)

The truth is the kindest thing we can give folks in the end.

Harriet Beecher Stowe (1811 - 1896)

Happily Saddened

A dog owns nothing, yet is seldom dissatisfied.

Irish Proverb

We would often be sorry if our wishes were gratified.

Aesop (620 BC - 560 BC)

Quantitative Retrospective

Where facts are few, experts are many.
> Donald R. Gannon

Hindsight is always twenty-twenty.
> Billy Wilder (1906 - 2002)

Measured Equally

We must use time as a tool, not as a crutch.
> John F. Kennedy (1917 - 1963)

Where all think alike, no one thinks very much.
> Walter Lippmann (1889 - 1974)

Engraved Indifference

Speak clearly, if you speak at all; carve every word before you let it fall.
> Oliver Wendell Holmes (1809 - 1894)

Nothing is more conducive to peace of mind than not having any opinions at all.
> Georg Christoph Lichtenberg (1742 - 1799)

Satisfied Loser

I have learned that to be with those I like is enough.
> Walt Whitman (1819 - 1892)

I'm better than dirt. Well, most kinds of dirt, not that fancy store-bought dirt... I can't compete with that stuff.
> Matt Groening (1954 -)

Mutual Outcome

Science without religion is lame, religion without science is blind.

Albert Einstein (1879 - 1955)

Mankind must put an end to war or war will put an end to mankind.

John F. Kennedy (1917 - 1963)

Surviving More

Out of life's school of war: What does not destroy me, makes me stronger.

Friedrich Nietzsche (1844 - 1900)

A hero is no braver than an ordinary man, but he is braver five minutes longer.

Ralph Waldo Emerson (1803 - 1882)

Fresh Focus

You're never too old to become younger.

Mae West (1892 - 1980)

Concentration comes out of a combination of confidence and hunger.

Arnold Palmer (1929 - 2016)

Adjusted Idealist

Only the hand that erases can write the true thing.

Meister Eckhart (1260 - 1327)

An optimist is the human personification of spring.

Susan J. Bissonette

Persistent Fable

Knowledge comes, but wisdom lingers.

Alfred Lord Tennyson (1809 - 1892)

Every man's life is a fairy-tale written by God's fingers.

Hans Christian Andersen (1805 - 1875)

Existing Elsewhere

We live in a Newtonian world of Einsteinian physics ruled by Frankenstein logic.

David Russell

God is not dead but alive and well and working on a much less ambitious project.

Anonymous

Loathing Idiot

Few people can be happy unless they hate some other person, nation, or creed.

Bertrand Russell (1872 - 1970)

Let us be thankful for the fools. But for them the rest of us could not succeed.

Mark Twain (1835 - 1910)

Meaning Endurance

Examine what is said, not him who speaks.

Arab Proverb

Being a newspaper columnist is like marrying a nymphomaniac. It's great for the first two weeks.

Lewis Grizzard (1946 - 1994)

Pronoun Stroll

Art is I; science is we.

Claude Bernard (1813 - 1878)

I like long walks, especially when they are taken by people who annoy me.

Noel Coward (1899 - 1973)

Solitary Connection

All men's misfortunes spring from their hatred of being alone.

Jean De La Bruyere (1645 - 1696)

Well, if I called the wrong number, why did you answer the phone?

James Thurber (1894 - 1961)

Retaliation Imagination

An eye for an eye makes the whole world blind.

Mahatma Gandhi (1869 - 1948)

Love looks not with the eyes, but with the mind.

William Shakespeare (1564 - 1616)

Confidently Concealed

I am never afraid of what I know.

Anna Sewell (1820 - 1878)

The more you know, the less you need to show.

Anonymous

Ongoing Outburst

Revolution is not a onetime event.
Audre Lorde (1934 - 1992)

Of those who say nothing, few are silent.
Thomas Neill

False Arrogance

The worst tragedy for a poet is to be admired through being misunderstood.
Jean Cocteau (1889 - 1963)

He who speaks without modesty will find it difficult to make his words good.
Confucius (551 BC - 479 BC)

Dreamed Risk

He who has never hoped can never despair.
George Bernard Shaw (1856 - 1950)

Injustice anywhere is a threat to justice everywhere.
Martin Luther King Jr. (1929 - 1968)

Fixed Restrictions

Truth, like surgery, may hurt, but it cures.
Han Suyin (1917 - 2012)

Argue for your limitations and sure enough, they're yours.
Richard Bach (1936 -)

Displayed Controll

Some people like my advice so much that they frame it upon the wall instead of using it.

Gordon R. Dickson (1923 - 2001)

The highest proof of virtue is to possess boundless power without abusing it.

Lord Macaulay (1800 - 1859)

Joke Case

In the end, everything is a gag.

Charlie Chaplin (1889 - 1977)

Let your memory be your travel bag.

Alexander Solzhenitsyn (1918 - 2008)

Meaningful Excitement

The question should be, is it worth trying to do, not can it be done.

Allard Lowenstein (1929 - 1980)

To love what you do and feel that it matters how could anything be more fun?

Katharine Graham (1917 - 2001)

Sound Control

It is common sense to take a method and try it.

Franklin D. Roosevelt (1882 - 1945)

I must govern the clock, not be governed by it.

Golda Meir (1898 - 1978)

Moral Longevity

Genius is talent provided with ideals.

William Somerset Maugham (1874 - 1965)

To lengthen thy life, lessen thy meals.

Benjamin Franklin (1706 - 1790)

Tuff Act

I never lie because I don't fear anyone. You only lie when you're afraid.

John Gotti (1940 - 2002)

The secret of success is sincerity. Once you can fake that you've got it made.

Jean Giraudoux (1882 - 1944)

Inner Truth

Only as you do know yourself can your brain serve you as a sharp and efficient tool.

Bernard M. Baruch (1870 - 1965)

The first principle is that you must not fool yourself and you are the easiest person to fool.

Richard Feynman (1918 - 1988)

Consuming Speech

Man does not live by words alone, despite the fact that sometimes he has to eat them.

Adlai E. Stevenson Jr. (1900 - 1965)

I never lecture, not because I am shy or a bad speaker, but simply because I detest the sort of people who go to lectures and don't want to meet them.

Henry Louis Mencken (1880 - 1956)

Altered Interest

A mind once stretched by a new idea never regains its original dimension.

Oliver Wendell Holmes Jr. (1841 - 1935)

The only factor becoming scarce in a world of abundance is human attention.

Kevin Kelly

Deferred Progeny

Procrastination is the thief of time.

Edward Young (1683 - 1765)

Poverty is the parent of revolution and crime.

Aristotle (384 BC - 322 BC)

Discovered Collection

Critics search for ages for the wrong word, which, to give them credit, they eventually find.

Peter Ustinov (1921 - 2004)

History is indeed little more than the register of the crimes, follies and misfortunes of mankind.

Edward Gibbon (1737 - 1794)

Altering Outcome

Promise yourself to live your life as a revolution and not just a process of evolution.

Anthony J. D'Angelo

The greatest challenge to any thinker is stating the problem in a way that will allow a solution.

Bertrand Russell (1872 - 1970)

Earned Opulence

You don't have to die in order to make a living.
> Lynn Johnston (1947 -)

One must be poor to know the luxury of giving.
> George Eliot (1819 - 1880)

Hazardous Intelligence

An error is the more dangerous the more truth it contains.
> Henri-Frédéric Amiel (1821 - 1881)

A handful of patience is worth more than a bushel of brains.
> Dutch Proverb

Lingering Unprotected

So of cheerfulness, or a good temper, the more it is spent, the more it remains.
> Ralph Waldo Emerson (1803 - 1882)

The same refinement which brings us new pleasures, exposes us to new pains.
> Edward Bulwer-Lytton (1803 - 1873)

Painful Misgivings

Suffering is one very long moment. We cannot divide it by seasons.
> Oscar Wilde (1854 - 1900)

Humanity is acquiring all the right technology for all the wrong reasons.
> R. Buckminster Fuller (1895 - 1983)

Cohabit Well

The wolf also shall dwell with the lamb, and the leopard
shall lie down with the kid.
Bible, Isaiah xi. 6.

As for me, except for an occasional heart attack,
I feel as young as I ever did.
Robert Benchley (1889 - 1945)

Precisely Timed

Cocooned inside our private dramas we often don't realize life
is rolling by us like it should.
Waiter Rant, *Waiter Rant weblog, 08-29-06*

I showed my appreciation of my native land in the usual Irish
way by getting out of it as soon as I possibly could.
George Bernard Shaw (1856 - 1950)

Gifted Fuel

I am no more humble than my talents require.
Oscar Levant (1906 - 1972)

What makes the engine go? Desire, desire, desire.
Stanley Kunitz (1905 - 2006)

Positioning Chaos

United we stand, divided we fall.
Aesop (620 BC - 560 BC)

Without discipline, there's no life at all.
Katharine Hepburn (1907 - 2003)

Selective Intelligence

The man who doesn't read good books has no advantage over the man who can't read them.

Mark Twain (1835 - 1910)

I don't hire anybody who's not brighter than I am. If they're not brighter than I am, I don't need them.

Paul "Bear" Bryant (1913 - 1983)

Mimic Offering

When people are free to do as they please, they usually imitate each other.

Eric Hoffer (1902 - 1983)

I have given two cousins to war and I stand ready to sacrifice my wife's brother.

Artemus Ward (1834 - 1867)

Continuous Intervolves

I am Alpha and Omega, the beginning and the end, the first and the last.

Bible, *Revelation xxii. 13.*

There's no present. There's only the immediate future and the recent past.

George Carlin (1937 -2008)

Escape Trap

When the water reaches the upper level, follow the rats.

Claude Swanson (1862 - 1939)

A countryman between two lawyers is like a fish between two cats.

Benjamin Franklin (1706 - 1790)

Ancient Target

An aged man is but a paltry thing, a tattered coat upon a stick.
William Butler Yeats (1865 - 1939)

If the point is sharp, and the arrow is swift, it can pierce through the dust no matter how thick.
Bob Dylan (1941 -)

Philanthropy Everlasting

Too many have dispensed with generosity in order to practice charity.
Albert Camus (1913 - 1960)

Everything in the world may be endured except continued prosperity.
Johann Wolfgang von Goethe (1749 - 1832)

Mature Visitor

All these years I've been feeling like I was growing into myself. Finally, I feel grown.
Oprah Winfrey (1954 -)

The camera makes everyone a tourist in other people's reality, and eventually in one's own.
Susan Sontag (1933 - 2004)

Counseling Decisions

If Columbus had an advisory committee he would probably still be at the dock.
Arthur Goldberg (1908 - 1990)

In matters of style, swim with the current; in matters of principle, stand like a rock.
Thomas Jefferson (1743 - 1826)

Lost Recognition

If you don't know where you are going, any road will take you there.

> Lewis Carroll (1832 - 1898)

One single grateful thought raised to heaven is the most perfect prayer.

> G. E. Lessing (1729 - 1781)

Brief Dido

Vigorous writing is concise.

> William Strunk Jr. (1869 - 1946)

People who keep journals have life twice.

> Jessamyn West (1902 - 1984)

Cut Short

The deeper sorrow carves into your being the more joy you can contain.

> Kahlil Gibran (1883 - 1931)

There are occasions when it is undoubtedly better to incur loss than to make gain.

> Titus Maccius Plautus (254 BC - 184 BC)

Long Gasp

Behind every successful man there are usually a lot of unsuccessful years.

> Author Unknown

There would not be so many open mouths if there were not so many open ears.

> Bishop Hall (1574 - 1656)

Continuous Cycle

Life is an unbroken succession of false situations.
                                        Thornton Wilder (1897 - 1975)
Each person's life is lived as a series of conversations.
                                        Deborah Tannen (1945 -)

Twice Thrice

**Nine out of ten people who change their minds
are wrong the second time too.**
                                        Author Unknown
**When you point your finger at someone,
three fingers are pointing back at you.**
                                        Anonymous

Ample Competition

Faith must have adequate evidence, else it is mere superstition.
                                        Alexander Hodge
**No government can be long secure without formidable
opposition.**
                                        Benjamin Disraeli (1804 - 1881)

Overlooked Donation

It does not do to dwell on dreams and forget to live.
                                        J. K. Rowling (1965 -)
The habit of giving only enhances the desire to give.
                                        Walt Whitman (1819 - 1892)

Concerned Creator

The scars of others should teach us caution.

Saint Jerome (AD 374 – AD 419)

Every man is the architect of his own fortune.

Sallust (86 BC - 34 BC)

Perfectly Prepared

People forget how fast you did a job but they remember how well you did it.

Howard Newton

Everybody's a self-made man; but only the successful ones are ever willing to admit it.

Author Unknown

Anticipated Collection

To solve the problems of today, we must focus on tomorrow.

Erik Nupponen

I not only use all the brains that I have, but all that I can borrow.

Woodrow Wilson (1856 - 1924)

Compounded Vulnerability

It's a recession when your neighbor loses his job; it's a depression when you lose yours.

Harry S Truman (1884 - 1972)

Envy is like a fly that passes all the body's sounder parts, and dwells upon the sores.

Arthur Chapman

Intelligent Advancement

When you hire people that are smarter than you are, you prove you are smarter than they are.
R. H. Grant

There is a homely old adage which runs: "Speak softly and carry a big stick; you will go far."
Theodore Roosevelt (1858 - 1919)

Plowing Forward

Skiing combines outdoor fun with knocking down trees with your face.
Dave Barry (1947 -)

The chief obstacle to the progress of the human race is the human race.
Don Marquis (1878 - 1937)

Infrequent Exhibition

Happiness in intelligent people is the rarest thing I know.
Ernest Hemingway (1899 - 1961)

The little foolery that wise men have makes a great show.
William Shakespeare (1564 - 1616)

Pecking Duck

Behold the turtle. He makes progress only when he sticks his neck out.
James Bryant Conant (1893 - 1978)

Tis better to be silent and be thought a fool, than to speak and remove all doubt.
Abraham Lincoln (1809 - 1865)

Self Inflicted

No one can make you feel inferior
without your consent.

Eleanor Roosevelt (1884 - 1962)

Folly is often more cruel in the consequences
than malice can be in the intent.

Aldous Huxley (1894 - 1963)

Adding Insight

Dwelling on the negative simply contributes to its power.

Shirley MacLaine (1934 -)

He is happiest who hath power to gather wisdom from a flower.

Mary Howitt (1799 - 1888)

Selecting Prospects

Evil has to exist along with good, in order that moral choice
may operate.

Anthony Burgess (1917 - 1993)

The future is not something we enter. The future is something
we create.

Leonard I. Sweet

Thoughts Materialize

College isn't the place to go for ideas.

Helen Keller (1880 - 1968)

When the student is ready. . . the lesson appears.

Gene Oliver

Empty Collapse

A society that puts equality... ahead of freedom will end up with neither.

Milton Friedman (1912 - 2006)

Rejoice not at thine enemy's fall but don't rush to pick him up either.

Jewish Proverb

Victorious Advocate

One should always play fairly when one has the winning cards.

Oscar Wilde (1854 - 1900)

One needs to be slow to form convictions, but once formed they must be defended against the heaviest odds.

Mahatma Gandhi (1869 - 1948)

Elected Positioning

There are times when you have to choose between being a human and having good taste.

Bertolt Brecht (1898 - 1956)

It has been my observation that most people get ahead during the time that others waste.

Henry Ford (1863 - 1947)

Think Contrast

In order to improve the mind, we ought less to learn, than to contemplate.

Rene Descartes (1596 - 1650)

I'd rather be a failure at something I love than a success at something I hate.

George Burns (1896 - 1996)

Lethargic Creator

Indolence is sweet, and its consequences bitter.
Voltaire (1694 - 1778)
**Every portrait that is painted with feeling
is a portrait of the artist, not of the sitter.**
Oscar Wilde (1854 - 1900)

Hear Clear

With the gift of listening comes the gift of healing.
Catherine de Hueck (1896 - 1985)
**Nothing astonishes men so much as common sense and plain
dealing.**
Ralph Waldo Emerson (1803 - 1882)

Quick Choice

**Successful leaders have the courage to take action
where others hesitate.**
Author Unknown
**Nothing can so alienate a voter from the political system as
backing a winning candidate.**
Mark B. Cohen (1949 -)

Duck Flip

Who escapes duty, avoids a gain.
Theodore Parker (1810 - 1860)
In a mad world only the mad are sane.
Akira Kurosawa (1910 - 1998)

Nurtured Sole

Some are kissing mothers and some are scolding mothers, but it is love just the same.

Pearl Buck (1892 - 1973)

Take your life in your own hands and what happens? A terrible thing: no one to blame.

Erica Jong (1942 -)

Humdrum Substitute

The days just prior to marriage are like a snappy introduction to a tedious book.

Wilson Mizner (1876 - 1933)

For flavor, instant sex will never supercede the stuff you have to peel and cook.

Quentin Crisp (1908 - 1999)

Pointless Growth

What's the use of worrying? It never was worthwhile.

George Asaf (1880 - 1951)

In a nation ruled by swine, all pigs are upward mobile.

Hunter S. Thompson (1939 - 2005)

Succeeding Males

The only time you don't fail is the last time you try anything – and it works.

William Strong

On Monday mornings I am dedicated to the proposition that all men are created jerks.

H. Allen Smith (1907 - 1976)

Organized Knowledge

Individuals may form communities, but it is institutions alone that can create a nation.

Benjamin Disraeli (1804 - 1881)

As a general rule the most successful man in life is the man who has the best information.

Benjamin Disraeli (1804 - 1881)

Instrument Ready

Troubles are often the tools God fashions us for better things.

Henry Ward Beecher (1813 - 1887)

To stay ahead, you must have your next idea waiting in the wings.

Rosabeth Moss Kanter (1943 -)

Solo Broadcast

Let every man be respected as an individual and no man idolized.

Albert Einstein (1879 - 1955)

Times have not become more violent. They have just become more televised.

Marilyn Manson (1969 -)

Credit Few

I awoke this morning with devout thanksgiving for my friends, the old and the new.

Ralph Waldo Emerson (1803 - 1882)

We would worry less about what others think of us if we realized how seldom they do.

Ethel Barrett (1913 - 1998)

Focusing Flight

Concentration is my motto - first honesty, then industry, then concentration.

Andrew Carnegie (1835 - 1919)

It's all right to have butterflies in your stomach. Just get them to fly in formation.

Dr. Rob Gilbert

Contrasting Quantity

There is only one difference between a madman and me. I am not mad.

Salvador Dali (1904 - 1989)

A little learning is a dangerous thing but a lot of ignorance is just as bad.

Bob Edwards (1947 -)

Alien Quote

I do not know myself, and God forbid that I should.

Johann Wolfgang von Goethe (1749 - 1832)

I shall never be ashamed of citing a bad author if the line is good.

Seneca (5 BC - AD 65)

Fatal Correctness

Gold is worse poison to a man's soul, doing more murders in this loathsome world, than any mortal drug.

William Shakespeare (1564 - 1616)

The difference between the right word and the almost right word is the difference between lightning and a lightning bug.

Mark Twain (1835 - 1910)

Alteration Fabrication

The need for change bulldozed a road down the center of my mind.
Maya Angelou (1928 - 2014)

Those that think it permissible to tell white lies soon grow color blind.
Austin O'Malley

Marriage Divorce

There is no remedy for love but to love more.
Henry David Thoreau (1817 - 1862)

Sometimes a good exit is all you can ask for.
Sean Stewart, _Perfect Circle, 2004_

Original Encounter

The first human who hurled an insult instead of a stone was the founder of civilization.
Sigmund Freud (1856 - 1939)

You can discover more about a person in an hour of play than in a year of conversation.
Plato (427 BC - 347 BC)

Bearing Down

The tree is known by his fruit.
Bible, Matthew xii.332

Storms make oaks take deeper root.
George Herbert (1593 – 1633)

Fading Reflection

Fashion is something that goes in one year and out the other.
Unknown

Enjoy your own life without comparing it with that of another.
Marquis de Condorcet (1743 - 1794)

Mutual Opposition

The Lord gave, and the Lord hath taken away;
blessed be the name of the Lord.
Bible, *Job i. 21.*

I am against using death as a punishment.
I am also against using it as a reward.
Stanislaw J. Lec (1909 - 1966)

Place Trap

Woman was God's second mistake.
Friedrich Nietzsche (1844 - 1900)

Use your enemy's hand to catch a snake.
Persian Proverb

Rhythmically Logical

The dance is a poem of which each movement is a word.
Mata Hari (1876 - 1917)

Only exceptionally rational men can afford to be absurd.
Allan Goldfein

Desired Wisdom

Dreams are wishes your heart makes.

American Proverb

Experience is the name everyone gives to their mistakes.

Oscar Wilde (1854 - 1900)

Abundant Anticipation

It is impossible to enjoy idling thoroughly unless one has plenty of work to do.

Jerome K. Jerome (1859 - 1927)

No matter how old you are, there's always something good to look forward to.

Lynn Johnston (1947 -)

Natural Look

The major sin is the sin of being born.

Samuel Beckett (1906 - 1989)

Silence is the most perfect expression of scorn.

George Bernard Shaw (1856 - 1950)

Try Twice

I am always doing that which I can not do, in order that I may learn how to do it.

Pablo Picasso (1881 - 1973)

I once said cynically of a politician, 'He'll doublecross that bridge when he comes to it.'

Oscar Levant (1906 - 1972)

Precious Loyalty

Time is the most valuable thing a man can spend.
> Theophrastus (372 BC - 287 BC)

Be true to your work, your word, and your friend.
> Henry David Thoreau (1817 - 1862)

Devine Fabrication

Remember now thy Creator in the days of thy youth.
> Bible, *Ecclesiastes xii. 1.*

I guess sometimes you have to lie to find the truth.
> Scott Westerfeld (1963 -)

Enduring Demand

The surprising thing about young fools is how many survive to become old fools.
> Doug Larson (1926 - 2017)

A man too busy to take care of his health is like a mechanic too busy to take care of his tools.
> Spanish proverb

Totally Satisfied

Luck is what you have left over after you give 100 percent.
> Langston Coleman

Nobody got anywhere in the world by simply being content.
> Louis L'Amour (1908 - 1988)

Briefly Lengthy

Growth demands a temporary surrender of security.
Gail Sheehy (1937 -)
It takes a long time to bring excellence to maturity.
Publilius Syrus (~100 BC)

Intimate Intake

**You can't find any true closeness in Hollywood,
because everybody does the fake closeness so well.**
Carrie Fisher (1956 - 2016)
**I don't want someone shoving his views down my throat,
unless they're covered in a crunchy candy shell.**
Stephen Colbert (1964 -)

Corrupt Conclusion

Hate pollutes the mind.
Author Unknown
When a rose dies, a thorn is left behind.
Ovid (43 BC - AD 17)

Aging Over

No man loves life like him that's growing old.
Sophocles (496 BC - 406 BC)
It is tedious to tell again tales already plainly told.
Homer (800 BC - 700 BC)

Reluctant Passing

Always do what you are afraid to do.
> Ralph Waldo Emerson (1803 - 1882)

The best way out is always through.
> Robert Frost (1874 - 1963)

False Accusation

Nothing anyone says in a bar is true.
> Mark Ruffalo (1967 -)

I married beneath me - all women do.
> Nancy Astor (1879 - 1964)

Polite Appreciation

Good manners will open doors that the best education cannot.
> Clarence Thomas (1948 -)

It's not having what you want. It's wanting what you've got.
> Sheryl Crow (1962 -)

Familiar Attire

Let each man exercise the art he knows.
> Aristophanes (450 BC - 388 BC)

Beware of all enterprises that require new clothes.
> Henry David Thoreau (1817 - 1862)

Consuming Decadence

**A crust eaten in peace is better than
a banquet partaken in anxiety.**

Aesop (620 BC - 560 BC)

**To educate a man in mind and not in morals
is to educate a menace to society.**

Theodore Roosevelt (1858 - 1919)

Prior Understanding

Chew before you swallow.

George W. Bush (1946 -)

Grasp the subject, the words will follow.

Cato the Elder (234 BC - 149 BC)

Risk-takers Dream-makers

The future belongs to those who dare.

Anonymous

Readers are plentiful; thinkers are rare.

Harriet Martineau (1802 - 1876)

History Undone

The past is the only dead thing that smells sweet.

Edward Thomas (1878 - 1917)

A book of quotations . . . can never be complete.

Robert M. Hamilton

Printed in the United States
By Bookmasters